The Crab That Crawled
Out of the Past

LORUS & MARGERY MILNE

The Crab That Crawled Out of the Past

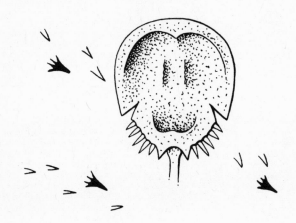

Drawings by Kenneth Gosner

ATHENEUM 1966 NEW YORK

To Keffer Hartline
who sees eye to eye with
horseshoe crabs

Contents

The Crab That Crawled
Out of the Past

The Fisherman's Find

THE OUTBOARD MOTOR coughed on its last breath of gasoline. Expertly, the fisherman jackknifed it, raising its still-whirling propeller out of the shallow water. The splash of his bow wave quieted to a hiss, then to a whisper, then to silence as his little boat lost speed. With a paddle the man held his course toward the sandy shore. There wavelets rose an inch or two, frothed along the edge, and fell back almost soundlessly.

Through the clear water the man watched for the few large stones he knew lay half-hidden amid the swaying blades of eelgrass. A dozen little killifishes took fright as his boat advanced above them. In a panic, they flashed by, glinting silver in the sunlight. As they vanished astern, the fishes disturbed the eelgrass blades. Periwinkle snails feeding on the eelgrass quickly released themselves. They drew back into the hard protection of their shells as they sank to the sandy bottom. For a few minutes the snails rolled there, shifted by the same energy that produced the waves along the shore. Then the snails regained confidence. They caught hold of the eelgrass and began to creep higher on the pliable blades to browse.

Five feet more to go, and the fisherman's boat would grate against the shore. Suddenly the man flashed his paddle. He swerved his boat to avoid hitting something dark brown he saw bulging upward from the sandy bottom. Then he laughed and leaped to the dry beach, keeping the bowline in his hand. That was no rock. It was just a harmless sea creature, which he recognized at once to be a horseshoe crab. As he hauled his boat up onto the sand, toward the trailer behind his parked car, he saw the crab turn and glide out toward deeper water in the bay.

For many minutes before the fisherman's boat arrived, the underwater world of the crab had throbbed with the exhaust sound of his outboard motor. It had not disturbed the crab. The animal had continued to shove its armored body forward slowly. It had flattened the eelgrass blades as a bulldozer might, knocking them down in a path a full eight inches wide. From the eelgrass the snails scattered in all directions. Frequently the horseshoe crab paused to eat. It gathered into its mouth a small snail, shell and all, or a squirming sea worm, or a bit of seaweed.

When the motor stopped, the underwater world of the crab had grown silent. Next had come the looming bulk of the fisherman's boat overhead. None of this had called upon the crab for any of the inborn reactions that protect its way of life. But when the shallow water had suddenly vibrated again with the double jolt of the man's feet on the shore and the harsh sound of his boat crunching into the sand, the

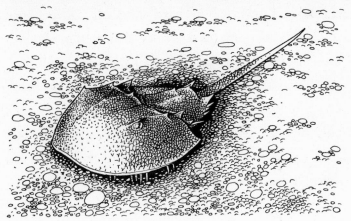

crab had pivoted on its ten legs and hurried away from the beach.

After the fisherman got his boat on its trailer and had it tied down all ready to travel, he returned to the water's edge to rinse his hands. Just offshore he saw several more horseshoe crabs in the sandy shallows. Some were only four inches across, others more than twelve. Every one of them trailed a tapering tail spine behind a body that resembled a metal wash basin upside down.

One crab crept along so close to shore that its brown back bulged out of the water and glistened in the sunlight. The man walked to the animal, seized it by its tail spine, and lifted it up for a better view. While hanging head downward, the crab could do little but wave its reddish brown legs. Whenever one leg bumped another, the armor that covered them clattered, showing how hard the shell was between joints in the legs. Within its armor, the animal's muscles and nerves and blood were well protected.

When the man turned the crab until its back faced him, its waving legs were hidden below its bulging body. The front two-thirds of its shell formed a single, almost circular piece. From its back, three sharp spines stood out, each like a miniature mountain. The spine toward the front of the body had a tiny lens on each side of it. Light passed through the lenses to a pair of minute eyes. With them the crab could tell night from day, could see how brightly the sun shone on its body—but little more. The other two spines, farther back on each side, seemed to shield from any harm the larger, oval eyes that were located there.

With a finger of his free hand, the fisherman touched one of these eyes and found it just as hard as the rest of the shell. The eye was immovable—fixed in the armored body. Yet, as the man looked at the eye, he could see in it a dark area that changed position whenever he turned the crab. He felt sure

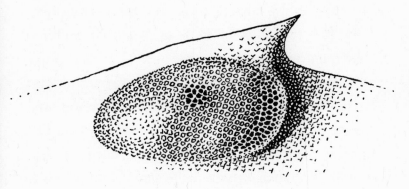

Eye of the horseshoe crab

that the crab was looking at him, and that this was the dark pupil of its eye. How, he wondered, could the pupil follow him while the eye itself did not move?

He turned the crab around and saw that this larger, front part of its body supported all of its waving legs. Curious, he thrust the tip of his little finger into the deep central groove between the bases of the legs. This was the crab's long, slit-shaped mouth. But in it he could feel no teeth or jaws. A horseshoe crab has no teeth or jaws at all. Unlike any other living animal, this crab grinds its food between the rough bases of its ten legs. The crab might be said to chew by rubbing all of its shoulders together, from the two sides of its long mouth. It couldn't bite the man's finger.

The crab continued to twist this way and that— trying to free its tail spine from the man's grasp. The tail spine itself was joined to the body by what seemed to be a ball-and-socket joint, one that permitted the crab to turn the tail in almost any direction. The tail spine arose from the last third of the body, which had a roughly triangular outline. The two sides of the triangle that came together at the tail joint resembled the teeth along the edge of a coarse saw. There were six notches between the teeth on each and in each of these was a short, movable spine, which appeared to serve only as a decoration.

The fisherman marveled that a creature whose armored body was in just two parts, hinged together, should be able to jerk so vigorously on the tapering tail spine he held. The crab kept doubling up and straightening out again. It bent its back at the hinge along the forward side of the triangular part of its body, opposite the tail. This trick threw its weight backward and forward. The man had to hold tight to prevent the crab from getting away.

He had measured and weighed many fishes while they were still wriggling. From his long experience he estimated the size of the horseshoe crab to be nine inches at its broadest, two inches thick from the undersurface to the highest area of the rounded body, eleven inches from front to back (not counting the tail spine), and eight inches for the tail spine itself. He judged the crab to weigh close to three pounds.

On its underside, between its tail spine and its legs, the crab had six thin, broad plates that overlapped like the shingles on a roof. The fisherman slipped his finger under the free edge of one of the plates and raised it toward him to see what lay beneath. He exposed a pair of soft organs with a

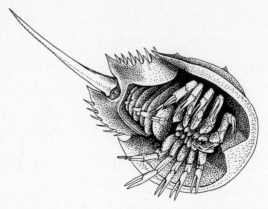

creamy yellow color. They were divided into fine vanes suggesting the red gills of a fish. The man guessed that the crab used them for breathing. He could feel the animal trying to cover these delicate organs, but the muscles with which it moved the thin overlapping plates were too weak to force his finger out. The crab arched its back at the hinge joint and pushed its gills and his finger within reach of its waving legs. He took his finger away, and the crab struggled less than while he was exploring its tender gills.

Holding the crab at arm's length, he reached out over the water and lowered the animal below the surface. The place he chose was deeper than he expected and, when he let go of the crab's tail spine, the creature sank to the sandy bottom upside down. It continued to wave its legs without being able to reach anything. The thin overlapping plates that protected its gills took up the rhythm. They and all five pairs of legs moved forward at almost the same time. Then the gill plate nearest the tail swung backward against the body. The next gill plate swung against it. And the next, and the next, and the next, and the next. The hindmost pair of legs swung toward the gill plates. One after another the pairs of legs followed suit, until all of them reached their farthest position toward the tail. Now all of the legs and gill plates swung forward for another spasm of activity.

For nearly a minute, the crab lay on its back, moving only its legs and gill cover plates. Then, suddenly, it turned its tail spine toward the bottom at almost a right angle from the body. It straightened the hinge joint between the larger forward part of its shell and the smaller, triangular part. Fascinated, the fisherman watched the horseshoe crab raise itself from the bottom in this way until it slowly toppled over sideways, falling on its feet, ready to creep away. So *that* was what the tail spine was for—to help the crab turn over when it fell on its back.

The fisherman had been bending over while he watched the crab so intently. Now he straightened his own back and turned toward his car. He wondered why he had never noticed this particular kind of crab in the bay before, although he had come there to fish many times.

From the shade of his boat on its trailer he picked up the yellow plastic bucket that held all of the flounders he had caught today. He looked at the fish, each with its eyes set close together and its mouth twisted. Certainly the appearance of the flounder was almost as strange, for a fish, as the horseshoe crab.

Then it occurred to him that each kind of sea life has its own season. Early spring was the time for smelt and alewives. Later came the striped bass and the salmon. Still warmer weather was good for flounder. Perhaps the horseshoe crabs too migrated toward shore regularly. It was July 1 and he hadn't actually fished in the bay before during July. Perhaps that was why the only horseshoe crabs he had met before were dead ones, whose bodies had been cast on the beach by storms. He had often picked up their dry shells and wondered how the animals acted while they were alive.

Now he knew.

The Horseshoe Crab's Way

ON A DOOR FRAME in many homes, a series of pencil marks with dates show how tall each child was on each birthday. Without this record, no one would know just how much growth had taken place from year to year.

At Wellesley College, a similar record was kept for nine years of a horseshoe crab growing in a big aquarium full of sea water. When first caught, the crab was only a little more than an inch and a half wide. In her ninth year of public life, she had grown to a width of eight inches. At this rate, she needed only two years more to reach the average size of mature female horseshoe crabs caught near shore along the Massachusetts coast. But something went wrong with her aquarium, and the record ended.

Most animals grow a little each day until they reach full size. A horseshoe crab does not. Instead it remains the same size for many months. Then it changes size quickly—in twenty-four hours or less. This is because it lives inside a hard shell. To grow, it must shed its protective armor. It does so, then expands to a new, larger size, and quickly produces another shell to shield it from harm. Usually a horseshoe crab makes the change while partly buried in the sandy bottom. There it is less likely to be attacked before its new armor hardens.

As the time for change in size comes near, usually in midsummer for crabs past the baby stage, the soft, living skin of the crab separates from the hard shell that covers it. Because the soft skin is ready to go around a larger body, it is puckered up into folds and wrinkles inside the old tight shell. Before long, the old shell cracks open all around the circular rim of the large, front part of the armored body. It is then that the crab digs itself into the sand as well as it can.

While partly buried, the crab swallows quantities of water, distending itself like a person after a big dinner. Slowly it crawls out of the slit around the rim of its shell, as though stepping out of its skin. As the crab escapes, it expands even more, to its new larger size and all the wrinkles in its skin are stretched out. Now the crab waits, motionless. Gradually the outer layer of its soft skin turns hard in contact with the sea water. Once more the horseshoe crab is armor-plated. But it is about a fourth larger in width and length and thickness than it was before.

Inside its new shell the animal has plenty of space for its muscles, its digestive system, and the other parts that were so cramped in the old shell. For perhaps five months the new shell actually will be too big for the animal. As though to keep from rattling around inside its armor, the crab fills up the shell with water—more water than there is real need for. Then, for a month or two, the crab and its shell will

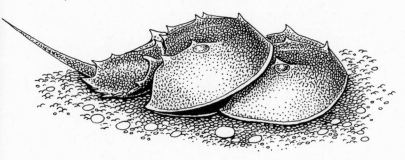

Crab shedding shell

match in size, and less water will be carried. After that, the crab becomes increasingly cramped, like a boy who has outgrown his clothes and is likely to split them open at every seam.

These changes go on inside the shell without much effect on the crab's weight. Its growing organs merely replace the extra water inside the shell. Only when the animal sheds its shell does its weight increase greatly. Just a few minutes after it escapes from its tight armor, the crab is about twice as heavy as it was before, from the extra water it swallows.

Usually, after a horseshoe crab sheds its hard shell, the shell remains partly buried in the sand of the sea bottom and decays there. But if a storm creates great waves, they are likely to shift the sand and expose the empty shell, then toss it on the beach. There it dries out and becomes brittle. A sharp-eyed beachcomber may pick it up and notice the slit around the rim of the front part. It would be easy to conclude that the crab had somehow crawled out of its own mouth—if the person looking at the shell did not know that the crab's mouth is actually underneath, between the bases of its walking legs.

Often the shed skins of horseshoe crabs seem to be in perfect condition. Even the slit around the rim may close as the shell dries. The finder of such a shell might then conclude that he held in his hand the dry remains of a complete animal, as though the hot sun had made it into a mummy. A dry skin of this kind reached England early in the seventeenth century and puzzled scientists there, who had never seen a horseshoe crab. One of them guessed that the oval transparent areas he saw in the larger part of the shell were windows to admit light into the spacious interior. These "windows" were actually the lenses of the compound eyes, which the crab replaces when it sheds its old shell.

By shedding its armor every year and exposing a new covering, a horseshoe crab gets rid of the many plants and animals that steal a ride on its back. Some of them are small seaweeds that resemble moss. They grow on the shell wherever the horseshoe crab does not scrub itself clean against the sand while digging in search of food. Limpets, which are snails with a shell shaped something like a coolie hat, hold tight to the crab while they browse on the seaweeds. Boat shells, which are snails that feed on tiny bits of food sucked in from the surrounding water, find places to cling on a horseshoe crab. Generally a boat shell or two can be found on a big crab underneath, near its gills and legs. Even barnacles and sea worms take up residence on the crab's shell and there build limy armor of their own. From this protection they reach out into the water for things to eat that are as small as dust particles. When a crab crawls out of its old shell, it leaves behind all of these hangers-on. Only the largest, oldest horseshoe crabs wear a load of clinging creatures. Perhaps these crabs have come to an age at which they can no longer grow a new shell each year.

To double its weight in twelve months, a horseshoe crab must hunt for food almost all the time. Slowly the animal creeps over the muddy and sandy bottom of the sea, into which it can thrust the sensitive, slender pincers on its walking legs. When it feels a worm or a clam, it gets a good grip and pulls out the creature it has caught. The crab's food is most often a clamworm or a ribbon worm, a razor clam or a soft-shell clam. But even a periwinkle snail is acceptable to a hungry horseshoe crab.

Whenever a crab is using several pincers at once to bring prey to its mouth, its legs work together as though they were parts of a machine. The rough "shoulders" take the food as it is handed to them, and maul or crush it before pressing it inward. Sand, pebbles, and bits of broken clam shell go along. Like a bird, the crab uses these hard objects to help its muscular gizzard grind its food into small pieces.

Usually the horseshoe crab spits out the bits of shell, the pebbles and coarse sand before the food goes on into its intestine to be digested.

While satisfying its continual need for food, a horseshoe crab is sensitive to other things in its world. It is aware of night and day, of storm and calm, of the time of year. At mating season, it responds also to the phases of the moon or to the particularly high tides that come at new moon and full moon.

After the sky becomes dark, horseshoe crabs of all ages go swimming. Perhaps this is the only time they can do so without being attacked by gulls and other sea birds. To change from creeping to swimming, a crab begins a slow run on the bottom. Rising as high as it can on its jointed legs, it bobs along in a way that suggests a heavy airplane taxiing over rough ground toward the end of the airport runway. Rhythmically, the legs and gill cover plates propel the animal forward. Suddenly the body tilts upward at the front, like an airplane taking off. But through this maneuver the crab achieves a backward somersault in slow motion. Legs and gill plates continue their beating. They drive the inverted crab along on a slanting course that rises gradually to the water surface. There the animal levels off and continues to swim, sometimes for several minutes. Then it rests and sinks slowly through the water, back downward.

If the crab resumes its rhythmic beat of feet and gill plates, it rises again to the surface and continues onward. Generally it follows one direction, as though it knew well where it was going and had a compass to steer by. Or the crab may sink all the way to the bottom. There it lands on its back and quickly uses its tail spine to turn over. Again the crab goes searching for food.

The basin-shaped body of the horseshoe crab fits it for swimming upside down rather than right side up. In this position it is streamlined, like the bow of a round-bottomed boat. Whenever the crab stops swimming and sinks toward the bottom, the same streamlining keeps its back downward. But once the animal rights itself and creeps into shallow water, its shell helps prevent the crab from being swept off its

Crab swimming

feet by waves. Each sidewise current of water goes up and over the horseshoe crab, pressing it against the bottom. No matter which way the water comes from, the effect is the same. This lets the crab travel in any direction with equal ease.

Many of the travels of horseshoe crabs go in definite directions. The animal has no magnetic compass, yet it need not wander at random. Even if a crab is lifted out of the water and carried up the beach, it does not lose its way. Once put down, it promptly turns and heads straight for the water. If it is carried back and set down a second time beside the first tracks it made toward the water, it sets out on a new course parallel to the first one. Slopes that rise toward the sea may slow its travels on land. Obstacles can distract it temporarily. Yet the animal shows a clear sense of direction—as long as it can use its large eyes and at least a third of the sky is clear of clouds. On an overcast day, or at night (unless the moon is bright), horseshoe crabs move about less freely. Often, they just dig in and wait for the sky to clear.

Until recently, no one knew how a horseshoe crab could tell direction. Then it was discovered that they detect certain patterns in the light from the sky, both on land and in the water world they ordinarily inhabit. Without special glasses made of Polaroid material, our eyes overlook these patterns. On a cloudy day, when the natural pattern in the sky is concealed, an artificial pattern can be provided for a horseshoe crab on a beach. If a large sheet of Polaroid material is held level just above the crab, the light from the cloudy sky passes through the Polaroid sheet and becomes polarized. The crab will promptly start off in some one direction. This direction changes if the Polaroid sheet is turned. Apparently horseshoe crabs learn that they reach deep water by keeping the pattern of light in one position. The opposite direction leads to shore.

The patterns in light to which a horseshoe crab responds are caused by the scattering of the sun's rays as they strike particles of dust. From dawn until dusk the patterns change continually, according to the position of the sun. To use the patterns as a kind of compass—a "sky compass"—a crab must be able to see them and also to know what time of day it is. It is easy to prove that the crab relies upon its large oval eyes to see the patterns. If these are covered with masking tape, the crab will not turn toward the shore as it will do when it can use its oval eyes. But so far no one has discovered where in its body the crab has the equivalent of a clock running on sun time. It *must* have one, to be able to use the sky compass so well at any hour of the day.

During its lifetime, each horseshoe crab makes at least one big journey. While very young, it lives near shore in shallow water. As it grows older and larger, it travels to deeper places in the ocean, places as much as seventy-five feet below the the surface. There, on muddy and sandy bottoms, it finds the sea worms and shellfish that are its favorite foods. Perhaps the crab escapes from the coldest weather by going deeper. If the temperature of the sea falls below 55 degrees Fahrenheit, the horseshoe crabs bury themselves in the bottom and wait for warmer weather.

To find out how far these crabs travel, Carl N. Shuster, Jr., attached metal tags with numbers to hundreds of horseshoe crabs on Cape Cod. He released the marked animals, just as bird banders do to learn where birds go. Some of the tagged crabs were caught again within two days. Others were discovered among unmarked crabs as much as two years later. One turned up twenty-one miles from the place where its tag had been attached. In fact, of the tagged crabs that were found again after they had been free for a month or more, only one was less than a mile from where it had been released. This one was nine-tenths of a mile down the coast.

The fishermen of Barnstable, Massachusetts, know that their town on the north shore of Cape Cod has about 13,500 human inhabitants, and that Barnstable Harbor is about a mile across and four miles long. But they had no way of telling whether their harbor was home to a thousand or a million horseshoe crabs. Carl Shuster gave them the answer after he studied the full-grown crabs he tagged and released there. Of the 327 marked crabs that he set free and did not see again during one summer and autumn, eight with tags turned up the following spring among 1,693 crabs examined. From this one experiment, it was possible to estimate that Barnstable Harbor contained between 50,000 and 100,000 adult horseshoe crabs. No way has been found to count the young crabs that live there, too.

Even so, there were far more horseshoe crabs than anyone had imagined.

More Horseshoe Crabs

As HORSESHOE CRABS become mature, the journey that has taken them into deeper water is reversed. They begin to travel back toward shallow water. By then they are nine to eleven years old and have shed their shells fifteen times or more.

Mature male crabs, which the fishermen call "bull" crabs, are smaller than most mature females (the "cow" crabs). The "bulls" usually reach the shoreline a few days before their mates. When both sexes have arrived and can be counted, about twice as many males are seen as females. Consequently, as each female crab approaches the beach, several suitors ordinarily hurry to her.

To find a mate, a male horseshoe crab does not need to use his eyes. In fact, on dark nights, a male can find a female just as easily as if it were daylight. It does not matter if the water is too muddy to see through. He seems to smell some special perfume coming from her through the water and goes directly toward its source. Adult males will run rapidly along the bottom to the place where a few gallons of sea water have been emptied, if the water has previously been used for washing a few mature "cow" crabs. Their perfume is still in the water.

People can tell a male horseshoe crab from a female without being able to smell the difference. On his front pair of walking legs, a male has a special pincer shaped like a strong fist and thumb. It is quite different from the slender pincer to be found on his other walking legs and on the front pair of walking legs of a female horseshoe crab.

With his two special fists and thumbs, a male can grip firmly the large saw teeth at either side of the tail spine of another crab. He uses these pincers to grasp and hold a female crab, if he can reach one before another male does. The female drags him along after her, like a trailer behind a car, until she

Crabs mating

is ready to lay her eggs. Although the male is still supporting his weight on his own feet, he keeps in position behind his mate only by holding tightly. Afterward, it is often possible to see where his special pincers gripped, for they leave a mark on the female's shell.

Often a suitor who hurries to a particularly fragrant female finds that she already has a partner. He may try to displace the male who already has hold of her saw teeth. Losing out, he may attach himself to the saw teeth of the male's shell. Then the female must pull along not just one male but two. Occasionally, a big female is seen with three or four males behind her, each attached to the next, the whole array looking like the tail on a kite.

Mated pairs and suitors searching for females are most conspicuous close to shore when the tide is high near full moon or new moon in early summer. Then the sea comes farther up on the beach than it is likely to again for another two weeks.

The heavy female, with her partner holding fast, searches for a suitable place for her eggs. At the very limit of high tide, she uses her walking legs and the curving front of her shell to dig into the sand. In the shallow nest she prepares, she lays two to three hundred eggs, each about an eighth of an inch in diameter. Her attached mate (or mates) seem to smell a new fragrance in the water and begin releasing the fluid that will fertilize her eggs and start them developing into baby horseshoe crabs.

A big female starts out with about a quart of eggs. She digs one nest after another until she has deposited them all. Often the tide begins to go out before she has filled more than one nest and covered it with sand. Then she and her mate leave the beach and try again at the next high tide. Sometimes they have come so far up the beach that they are stranded by the receding tide. Then they simply burrow into the mud or sand, and hide until the water returns.

The eggs of horseshoe crabs are eaten by many animals. A female crab who is laying eggs may be attended by more than her mate. A dozen minnows may swim right under the crabs' bodies to get the eggs, and leave only when they are so full that they can hold no more. Sometimes an eel slithers under a mated pair of crabs and devours the eggs as fast as the female lays them. On the Gulf Coast of Florida, catfish sometimes form a rosette around each pair of crabs in shallow water. Pushing against one another and lashing the surface into a foam, the catfish reach under the female crab, even when this position raises their tails into air. Despite the commotion, the crab continues to lay her eggs as though all were calm.

With so many pairs of crabs digging nests along the shore, vast numbers succeed in getting the eggs laid and covered over without being eaten. But by day sharp-eyed shore birds, such as plovers and sandpipers, find some nests that are poorly hidden. The birds open the nests and feast on eggs. In the first twenty-four hours, perhaps half of the eggs that the horseshoe crabs lay are destroyed. The others continue to develop in the wet sand.

A gentle rain will dilute the sea water that rises to the eggs between the sand grains but does no harm to the eggs. The sun warms the beach and transforms

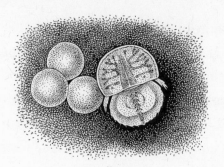

Larval crab

the hidden nests into incubators, in which the baby crabs can develop rapidly. But danger lies in violent storms that bring waves crashing high on the beach and wash out the nests full of young before it is time.

In a few days, if all goes well, the tough opaque covering of each egg cracks open. Out of it a thin, transparent balloon, containing the baby crab, escapes into the water between the sand grains. Within this delicate covering, which resembles a cellophane showcase, the crab can be watched as it grows. It sheds its skin twice before hatching. Its legs become distinct and begin to wave almost continuously. In less than two weeks, the baby animal reaches a stage at which it is ready to hatch. But it progresses no further unless waves churn up the nest. Ordinarily this happens at the high tide just two weeks after the eggs are laid. Sand grains moved by the water cut through the thin covering, and free the baby horse-shoe crab. Waves wash it toward the open sea or toss it on the beach.

Millions of baby crabs survive this rough treatment. But they are not yet out of danger. They must still escape being eaten before they reach the comparative safety of a sand bar. Once there they dig in and continue their development for several days. During this time they have no need to eat, for their tiny bodies still contain nourishing yolk that was left over from their life inside the egg.

At high tide, while the sea covers the sand bar with quiet water, the baby crabs often creep up through the sand. They swim a little and practice turning over onto their feet. At first this is difficult, for they have no tail spine to help them. After another molt, the tail spine begins to project and can be used when the crab rights itself.

While the baby crabs live in the surface layers of the sand bar, their color is almost the same as that of the sand. Birds walk over the sand bar at low tide, and fishes swim over it at high tide, without seeing the crabs that are hiding in the sand. People walk on the sand bar without hurting the little crabs or knowing that they are there. Yet, if a few spoonfuls of the surface sand are washed through a fine wire mesh (such as window screen), the baby crabs are left exposed. When freed into the water, they quickly settle to the bottom and burrow into the sand again.

For a young horseshoe crab, the first three years of life are the most dangerous. By the end of its first year, the little animal is about an inch across. Counting the twice that it shed its skin before hatching from its eggshell, it has molted seven times. Seven times it has doubled its weight. But its sand-colored armor is still too thin to give much protection from a fish's jaws or a gull's sharp beak. If the young crab exposes itself in water where large fishes swim, it is likely to be eaten. If it hunts for food in the surface mud at low tide in full daylight, a gull may wade to it and eat it.

Thousands of year-old horseshoe crabs are devoured in the shallows and sloughs of the coastal beach. Thousands more survive for two more years and four more changes to a larger size. After the third year, they are three inches across. Their armor is harder, darker brown, and protects them well. By then they are already beginning their slow migration into deeper parts of the sea where birds can no longer reach them. From the third year on, the growing crabs will change size only once a year, and grow up much more slowly. Only when they become mature will they return to the shore.

Out of the Distant Past

WHEN ONE FIRST meets a live horseshoe crab, the animal seems almost as unbelievable as the legendary Loch Ness monster or a real aardvark. It is completely different from every other creature. Until the end of the nineteenth century, even scientists did not know how this "crab" fitted into the family trees of the Animal Kingdom. It isn't really a crab at all.

Of the million kinds of animals alive today, only the horseshoe "crabs" chew their food with the spiny shoulders of all their walking legs. Only the horseshoe "crabs," when they shed their hard shell, grow a complete new set of lenses for their compound eyes. No other kind of animal has booklike gills under the second part of its body. Or ends in a long, stiff tail spine. Except for horseshoe crabs, no animal with these features has been found among the fossils from the past 230 million years.

Two hundred and thirty million years ago is far, far back in time. It is almost half of the immense history of the Earth since animals first began leaving their shells and their tracks in sediments that turned into rock. Yet, for an equal length of time before, the ancestors of horseshoe crabs had neighbors that were truly close kin. These relatives are called sea scorpions or eurypterids.

From about 425 million to 230 million years ago, when sea scorpions were alive, the ancestor of today's horseshoe crabs were never more than nine or ten inches long, counting the tail spine. Like the modern crab, the front part of its body had a circular outline suggesting a horse's hoof, curving to two points like a horseshoe. Below the second part of the body were the booklike, overlapping gills. But in the ancient horseshoe crab, this second part was not one solid piece of armor. It was divided crosswise into several pieces, hinged together, making the animal flexible. Yet, just as an athlete holds his body tense while diving into the water, the horseshoe crab could keep the hinged pieces from bending while it used its tail spine to turn right side up, after falling on its back.

Most sea scorpions also had tapered bodies. They were so flexible that they could turn their stiff tail spines in all directions—even up over their backs. A sea scorpion could use its sharp tail spine as a dagger. By curving the flexible second part of its body, a sea scorpion could bring the tip of the tail spine forward over its back and stab it into any struggling animal it had caught to eat. The spine was a good dagger; but it was not a stinger, like the sharp, curved tail spine on a land scorpion, because it had no poison.

The pincers of a sea scorpion were at the end of the front pair of walking legs. Each pincer was like that of a lobster, and must have been useful to hold prey. Often the fourth pair of walking legs on a sea

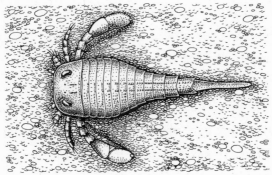

Sea Scorpion

scorpion had the form of long paddles or oars. The sea scorpion may have used these legs both for swimming and for steadying itself against the bottom of the lake or marsh while it held a struggling victim in its pincers.

Even the smallest sea scorpions grew to be at least six inches long. And some attained huge size—as much as nine feet long. No other animal without a backbone to strengthen its body has ever become so gigantic and so powerful. Some perhaps were even able to crawl out on land. Yet sea scorpions were like horseshoe crabs in that they chewed their food with spiny shoulders on their walking legs. They grew a complete new set of lenses for their compound eyes whenever they shed their shells. And usually they breathed with booklike gills below the second part of their flexible bodies.

The farther back scientists trace the fossil record of sea scorpions and horseshoe crabs, the more the one resembles the other. The most ancient horseshoe crab had a smaller first part of the body than do more modern ones. In this way it was more like the sea scorpions. The most ancient sea scorpion had a shorter second part of the body, and it appears that it was no more flexible there than an ancestral horseshoe crab. It is likely that about 600 million years ago there was no difference at all. At that time, some one kind of creature could have been the ancestor of both the later horseshoe crabs and also the sea scorpions.

The time when ancestral horseshoe crabs first appear as fossils in ancient rocks is known as the Cambrian period and is the earliest time from which scientists can really study living creatures. They know that there was life in the seas of the world long before this period, but the early creatures left little record of what they were like, probably because they were simple and quite small.

In the Cambrian period our world was utterly different from the world we know. The great continents had unfamiliar shapes. Their land was just bare rock, or gravel banks and sand bars. It had no soil, no plants, and no animals. The wind and the rivers shifted the sand from place to place. Strong currents of water carried along boulders and gravel, only to deposit them where the channel broadened or the slope of the land grew more gradual. In the great seas were many forms of life, none of them with backbones, but some of them quite large, and all of them seemingly numerous. They have been preserved as fossils for us to see by sediments that covered and smothered some of them, and then changed them to rock that has lasted through the millions of years down to the present.

In the shallow parts of the oceans, near shore, the horseshoe crabs fought for life with their many back-boneless neighbors. The earliest snails to produce a spiral shell were there. They probably fed on sea-weeds. The first clams sucked in sea water and strained tiny creatures from it as food. But except for these ancient kinds of horseshoe crab, the only common neighbors with paired legs were the trilobites—active little creatures that became extinct about 230 million years ago.

Following the Cambrian period came the period known as the Ordovician period. It is during early Ordovician times that sea scorpions first appear in fossil remains, in what appear to have been fresh-water lakes and shallow ocean ponds and marshes. From study of other living things that became fos-silized then, it is known that during these times all of the plants were still aquatic, some like pond scums and others like seaweeds. The first sea urchins were beginning to appear. The earliest known coral and sea lilies were reaching out their tentacles to capture small animals swimming by. And an even newer kind of creature was developing, some in the ocean and some in fresh-water lakes and estuaries. This was

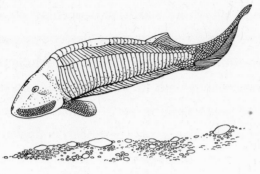

Jawless armored fish

a strange armored fish with no jaws, but with a back-bone. Like its spineless companions, it sucked water containing aquatic plants into its small round mouth. Meanwhile, the older forms, the horseshoe crabs and the trilobite, went on. The latter became food for the newly developed sea scorpions.

About 425 million years ago, the Ordovician period ended and the Silurian period began. It was during Silurian times that sea scorpions attained their largest size. Their neighbors included new reef-forming corals, sea stars, giant sea lilies, and more trilobites. But into the estuaries and the oceans from fresh water came a new kind of fish—the first one with jaws. Probably these fish competed with sea scorpions for trilobites as food. Gradually the number of trilobites and of sea scorpions grew smaller and smaller and the number of fishes with jaws in-creased.

But something else was happening to a distant relative of the sea scorpion, a descendant perhaps of an ancestor of the first sea scorpions. Along the edges of fresh water, both in wet places and on land, this relative was changing very gradually. Its tail spine disappeared. The second part of its body was a single piece, with no joints to give it flexibility. The relative of the sea scorpion was becoming the first land scorpion, and from its descendants eventually would come the first spiders.

By 405 million years ago, when the Silurian period was replaced by the Devonian period (the Age of Fishes), the seas were full of fishes. A few were as much as thirty feet long, with great biting jaws. Some were the ancestors of sharks, and others of the bony fishes that are more familiar today. And in early Devonian times, too, the first shrubby plants began growing on land, and the first insects began

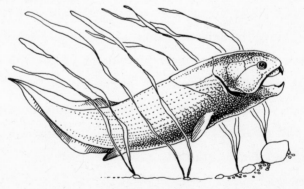

Devonian fish

chewing on the new land plants. There to eat the insects were the land scorpions and the spiders. The land scorpions and spiders represent the only living relatives of the horseshoe crab today, and they are very distantly related. For, after Devonian times, the numbers of sea scorpions decreased greatly, and by 230 million years ago there were no more to be found.

No one fears that the horseshoe crabs will be left with no relatives at all, however. Spiders feed mostly on insects, and have followed their prey all over the world. Land scorpions are found in some of the driest deserts. Spiders are among the few small animals that live in Antarctica. At the topmost peak of the highest mountains, spiders spin their silken webs as insect traps. So as long as there are insects, it seems likely that land scorpions and spiders will survive, too.

Somehow the horseshoe crabs were better fitted to survive than the original sea scorpions were. The crabs never grew to be more than about thirty inches long. But they managed to walk at their slow pace all the way from the shallow seas of Europe long ago to the Atlantic Coast of America and to the south shore of New Guinea in the East Indies. And there they continue to swim and creep along the bottom, finding enough to eat.

During the millenniums that followed the Devonian period, the crabs changed ever so slowly, developing into the form we see today. Yet in each million years the change was slight, and their habits in living changed even less. Then, as now, the crabs traveled every year to beaches of mud and sand to breed. And far faster than the crabs changed, the location of the beaches shifted. Seas flooded in over the continents, leaving sediments to harden into limestone and sandstone. The water drained off again as the continents rose.

It is almost incredible how much the shape of the continents changed, and the ocean outlines changed, and most of the living neighbors of horseshoe crabs changed, without affecting the crabs. During Devonian times, some of the fishes in fresh water—the lobe fins—seem to have developed lungs and then legs. Gradually they became the first amphibians—the ancestors of salamanders, frogs, and toads. In the ocean shallows, the fortunes of trilobites, sea scorpions and fishes with jaws went down or up. But none of these changes had much effect on the horseshoe crabs, or on their regular summer travels to shore to mate and lay their eggs.

As the Carboniferous period followed the Devonian, the plants on land began growing to tree size. At first all of them were giant ferns and club mosses and horsetails, many of them more than 120 feet tall. Among these trees in the swamps, insects became abundant. Scorpions and spiders and amphibians caught the insects. Plants grew faster than they decayed, and the remains of dead plants accumulated to form coal. The shape of the oceans and seas kept changing. But none of the new features did much to alter life for horseshoe crabs. On land a new type of animal with a backbone—the reptiles—appeared. But this meant nothing in the shallow seas while the Coal Ages (Carboniferous times) came and went.

Carboniferous reptile

Geologists can draw maps to show how the seas drained off the continents after the Coal Ages during Permian times, until the number of beaches was far smaller. On land the weather changed, with less rain and more drought. For the tree ferns and giant club mosses and great horsetail trees, and for the old-style amphibians, this meant disaster. For reptiles, it mattered very little. Reptiles now caught the insects that the amphibians had once eaten. On the drier land, cone-bearing trees began to replace the forests of giant ferns and other plants that needed great quantities of water. The sea scorpions became extinct. So did the ancient armored fishes. Even the number of horseshoe crabs decreased.

The Age of Reptiles (Mesozoic Era) began. Reptiles were scaly animals of the land, although some entered the seas to get fishes to eat. Like a bursting skyrocket they evolved in many directions at once. Those known as pterosaurs and pterodactyls took to the air, perhaps to catch insects. As dinosaurs, the reptiles walked and lumbered over the land and into every swamp. Or they pounced on one another. But, except for the reptiles that entered the shallow seas, none of these changes on land meant much to the horseshoe crabs.

There were horseshoe crabs all through the Age

Tyrannosaurus

of Reptiles. They crept along near shore during the first period, called the Triassic, when all of the reptiles were fairly small. The crabs followed their ancient ways during the second period, the Jurassic, which is the time of *Brontosaurus,* the famous "thunder lizard." This enormous reptile reached a total length of eighty feet or more, counting its long tail and long neck. Probably *Brontosaurus* kept most of its tremendous body submerged in a coastal lagoon while reaching out its small head on its long neck, to feed on seaweeds close to shore. It may often have disturbed a horseshoe crab that was running along the bottom in those same shallows.

On land, a terrifying dinosaur named *Allosaurus* stood fourteen feet high when it reared up on its powerful back legs. Half as long as a *Brontosaurus,* it hunted for smaller reptiles and pounced on them, to tear them apart with its ferocious jaws and eat their meat. Among its neighbors was *Stegosaurus,* a dinosaur that ate only plants and probably remained most of its time in swamps and coastal marshes where just its armored back was exposed to sun and air. Great triangular plates projected from its back, fending off the large meat-eating dinosaurs.

If a horseshoe crab ventured too far from shore, it could have been attacked by fish-eating reptiles

Ichthyosaur

that swam through the seas. These *Ichthyosaurs* resembled giant porpoises, and some were as much as thirty feet long. They must have been as ferocious as the big sharks that lived in the same oceans.

Probably most of the reptiles of Mesozoic times were far smaller and crept or walked or hopped along the ground. A few of these had leathery wings and flew about. Small ones might have resembled sparrows in armor, for they were clad in thin overlapping scales instead of feathers.

All around the horseshoe crabs the kinds of life were changing. But it did not matter to the crabs that the soft-bodied sea worms they ate were of new kinds, or that the small shellfish were constructed differently, or that the seaweeds were not quite the same. It was on the land, not in the shallow coastal seas, that some of the reptiles in the Jurassic period gained a new ability: to control automatically their

GEOLOGIC INTERVALS

MILLIONS OF YEARS	ERAS	PERIODS
1	CENOZOIC	Quaternary
		Tertiary
100	MESOZOIC	Cretaceous
		Jurassic
200		Triassic
	PALEOZOIC	Permian
300		Carboniferous
		Devonian
400		Silurian
		Ordovician
500		Cambrian
600		

AGES OF ANIMAL LIFE

own body temperature. These "warm-blooded" animals became, in the Cretaceous period, the first birds and first mammals. But the horseshoe crabs were unaffected; as they were when the seed ferns, which had been wide-spread for 220 million years, died out in the Jurassic and left their places on land to the cone-bearing trees, such as pines.

During the Cretaceous period, with which the Age of Reptiles came to an end, the dinosaurs suffered one catastrophe after another. Soon they were extinct altogether. In the watery world of horseshoe crabs at the same time, one group of coastal neighbors—the sea mollusks known as ammonoids—gave up making simple chambered, spiral shells. Although shells of this style had sheltered their ancestors for 325 million years, they suddenly began putting in partitions of amazing complexity. This may have been their downfall, for by the end of the Age of Reptiles, the ammonoids became extinct. Horseshoe crabs were unaffected. Nor did it matter to them that insects were going into a new partnership with plants, getting nectar and pollen from the first flowers, and helping set the seeds inside the first real fruits.

After the Age of Reptiles ended, about 63 million years ago, the Age of Mammals, or the Cenozoic Era, began. It was also the Age of Flowering Plants, and some of them—chiefly the grasses—spread over dry uplands where almost no vegetation had been able to survive before. New kinds of grazing mammals and seed-eating birds followed into the first prairies. The mammals became able to subsist on even the dry hay that remained during droughts when the grasses turned brown and stopped growing. These changes helped insects to find a living farther and farther from the sea. Land scorpions and spiders followed the insects. But the sea creatures, such as horseshoe crabs, had no part in all these alterations in the world of dry land.

The ways of horseshoe crabs had no need to change when, about two million years ago, another new kind of creature—man—began to leave indications of his presence among the sediments that preserved a fossil record.

It was not until within the last few centuries, in fact, that man got around to wondering scientifically about horseshoe crabs. The twentieth century A.D. had already begun when the famous British zoologist Edwin Ray Lankester discovered that horseshoe crabs are related more closely to modern land scorpions and spiders than to any other creature alive, though the relationship is distant. His interest in the fossil record, in comparing animals and in tracing the development of their embryos, began while he was still a boy. It led to his first scientific publication, about an armored jawless fish of Ordovician times, when he was just sixteen years old.

Later, Dr. Lankester studied almost every group of animals, and helped identify the proper place for each in the Animal Kingdom. For this he received the gold medal of the Royal Society of London, and the Darwin-Wallace medal of the respected Linnaean Society. When he retired as director of natural history at the British Museum, he was knighted by King Edward VII. Despite all these honors and the work that earned them, Sir E. Ray Lankester always looked back with particular pride upon having learned where the horseshoe crab belonged. To him they had walked right out of the distant past into modern times.

Who Made the Tracks?

In Bavaria, near the Alps in southeastern Germany, men have been quarrying a particularly fine-grained limestone for many years. On pieces of this stone, artists can make lithographs of the highest quality. In many of the slabs of limestone, the quarry men discover remains of animals from long ago. About 120 million years have passed since the animals lived and died, and were preserved in the fine grains of lime that became limestone.

Two of these fossils are among the most famous in the whole world. Found only about eight hundred feet apart (one in 1861, the other in 1956), they are of the earliest known bird. Named *Archaeopteryx,* it was about the size of a crow. In the Bavarian limestone the imprint of its feathers is well preserved. Many of its bones are in place, just where they were when the bird died. The feet are fitted for both walking and perching. But, unlike modern birds, *Archaeopteryx* had sharp teeth in both jaws, instead of a horny beak. Its tail was long and jointed, with feathers on both sides. Although clearly a bird, the creature is also a "glorified reptile."

Often, when slabs of the Bavarian limestone are split apart, the tracks of ancient animals are also found. Scientists believe that these footprints and trails were made by live animals as they walked or crept over the wet beach of a quiet, shallow lagoon. The fine particles of lime that composed the beach were accumulating in layers under the gentle action of small waves. The weight of an animal pressed the lime particles together firmly, and this slight difference was preserved when the particles became united into limestone rock.

Similar tracks can be seen on mudflats and sea beaches today, where gulls and other birds have walked, or where sea turtles have come ashore to lay their eggs. Beachcombers often try to guess what kind of creature made each pattern along the shore. Fossil tracks, such as those in the Bavarian limestone, provide a still greater challenge to scientists, who would like to know what animals patrolled the shores so long ago. Some of the marks in the limestone might be footprints of *Archaeopteryx,* made as the bird walked along the edge of a lagoon in search of food. Other tracks may be footprints of different "glorified reptiles"—ancient birds for which no fossil remains have yet been found.

Just as the footprints of gulls, sandpipers, crabs, and sea snails all overlap along the edge of the water on a beach today, so too the fossil tracks seem to be on top of one another. The scientists have tried to sort them out, searching for patterns to match the animal life already known, and also for distinctive patterns made by birds no man has yet seen.

When scientists first began to study these tracks,

Archeopteryx

they needed to be able to talk about the different patterns and to keep notes on where each was found. So the scientists dreamed up names for the birds that probably made each kind of track. One received the fanciful name *Ornichnites caudata* because it left a mark by dragging its tail. Others became known as *Protornis bavarica* ("the ancient bird of Bavaria"), and *Hypernithes jurassica* ("the bird of the Jurassic period that walked on top of the other tracks"). The longest name of all went to *Kouphichnium lithographicum* ("the track maker of the lithographic limestone"). Everyone hoped that someday a fossil skeleton with feathers would be found to match each of these distinctive tracks.

Instead, in 1938, all of these different tracks led to an amazing discovery. Another slab of Bavarian limestone was split open. There were the overlapping patterns made by many feet, all beautifully preserved. And there, at the end of the tracks, where they all stopped at once, was a fossilized animal. It was a horseshoe crab.

Here was the imaginary "bird" *Ornichnites caudata,* which dragged its tail. With its first four pairs of walking legs, the crab had imprinted the lime particles with the tracks of the "ancient bird of Bavaria" (*Protornis bavarica*). And then, with its fifth pair of legs, it had added the distinctive pattern of the "bird of the Jurassic period that walked on top of the other tracks" (*Hypernithes jurassica*).

There is a good reason for the difference between the footprints of a horseshoe crab's first four pairs of walking legs and those of its fifth pair. The first four pairs end in sharp-pointed pincers which are kept closed while walking. The fifth pair are "pushers." They operate on the same principle as a ski pole. Instead of a ring placed back of the sharp tip to prevent the pole from going far into the snow, the crab's fifth pair of walking legs bear several hinged flaps that open at right angles. They stop the legs from sinking into the bottom when the crab uses these legs to push itself along.

Horseshoe crabs had also made the distinctive trail of the "track maker of the lithographic limestone" (*Kouphichnium lithographicum*). This pattern

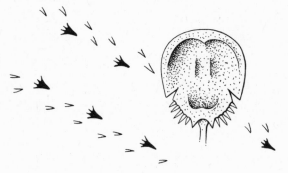

Fossil tracks

showed where a mated pair of crabs had walked in tandem. The horseshoe crabs that left all these trails behind them were not even members of an unknown or rare kind. They were just plain *Mesolimulids,* which geologists know as the commonest horseshoe crab during the Triassic and Jurassic parts of the Age of Reptiles—perhaps 75 million years. For all this time, it was widespread. Now it is regarded as the greatest track maker in all history.

Long before the dinosaurs became extinct, *Mesolimulids* seem to have spread over many of the world's shallow seas. Already they had a flat-bodied cousin (*Limulus syriaca*) in the Near East. By the end of the Jurassic they had other relatives, of one kind or another, in the Far East and in North America. Some form of horseshoe "crab"—perhaps even our present-day form, *Limulus polyphemus*—was crawling and swimming in our eastern coastal waters at the time of the last great dinosaurs and of the first-known plants with flowers. It was there before the Rocky Mountains were formed, before the Andes or the Alps or the Himalayas. Few animals that a beachcomber can find in America have remained essentially unchanged for so long.

Wherever it crawls on a mudflat that is exposed to air or covered by only an inch of water, a horseshoe crab is likely to leave its characteristic tracks. Unless its body is buoyed up by water, its feet dig in and its tail drags behind. Probably horseshoe crabs have been making marks in this way ever since these animals first appeared on earth. To learn whether any other tracks known to science might have been made by horseshoe crabs—as those in the Bavarian limestone were—an outstanding geologist at the University of Cincinnati led a search into the past. Dr. Kenneth E. Caster investigated as far back as Devonian times in the Age of Fishes, perhaps 360 million years ago.

Sedimentary rocks of this age from Pennsylvania contained tracks that previous scientists had been unable to match with any animal they knew. In Devonian times, the scientists felt sure, a halfway creature, halfway between fishes and amphibians, existed. It must have been something that half swam and half walked, and perhaps made scratchy marks and tail prints along the bottom. These habits would go with a creature halfway between the lobe-fin fishes of still earlier times and the first amphibians, which came late in the period. To the imagined animal and the real tracks in the Pennsylvania rocks the scientists had given the name *Paramphibius*.

Dr. Caster had good reason to suspect that the

the *Paramphibius* tracks did not belong to the halfway creature, for they were associated with fossils of sea animals. By contrast, the first amphibians and the lobe-fin fishes from which they supposedly evolved all lived in fresh water, just as salamanders and frog tadpoles do today. The halfway creature must have lived there, too.

When Dr. Caster compared the *Paramphibius* tracks with the feet of horseshoe crabs of Devonian times, he found that they fitted perfectly. He even got modern horseshoe crabs to make tracks on mud that were almost indistinguishable from the ancient footprints. This left the halfway creature, which surely existed, as much a mystery as ever.

Other scientists were inspired by Dr. Caster's success. They re-examined some tracks that had been found in sedimentary rocks of Greenland, and also two different trails from New Jersey. All of these footprints had been made during the Triassic period, at the beginning of the Age of Reptiles. The tracks in Greenland had been credited to some ancient amphibian that resembled a giant salamander and was heavily armored. Some of these had skulls four feet long. They made fine fossils and were known as stegocephalians ("armored-headed animals"). They were descendants of the mysterious halfway creature,

Stegocephalian

and appeared first during the great Coal Ages—the Carboniferous period. Later they reached still larger size, but became extinct in the late Triassic.

The tracks from New Jersey rocks of Triassic age were supposed to be the footprints of a small hopping dinosaur, or perhaps a creature with wings, such as a diminutive ancestor of the earliest birds. But when the tracks of horseshoe crabs were compared with the tracks in the Triassic rocks of New Jersey and those of Greenland, no one could tell them apart.

Perhaps any horseshoe crab can do as well at leaving imprints on the muds. For at least 500 million years, this one type of animal, in almost its present form, seems to have walked and swum along the edge of the sea. Its tracks have remained there as a message for man out of the distant past. But only recently has he learned to read the message.

Science began in Europe, where there are no living horseshoe crabs. Until recently few people who studied fossils traveled to the Far East or to the Atlantic Coast of America, where they might meet these strange animals. Not until the sixteenth century, in fact, did scientists discover the existence of horseshoe crabs. Many more years passed before anyone watched carefully to see how the crabs lived, what they ate, and what they left behind.

The Discovery of the
Se-ekanauk

THE FIRST ENGLISH colonists sailed to the New World just ninety-two years after Christopher Columbus discovered America. These ninety-one men and seventeen women were prepared to clear the land and settle a colony. They intended to build log houses for shelter, raise grain and other food, defend themselves against bands of Indians if necessary, and become acquainted with many strange plants and animals.

The vague country to which they came had been laid claim to and named the year before. Its boundaries were still unknown. Sir Walter Raleigh had called it Virginia, after Queen Elizabeth, the virgin queen, when in 1584 the two ships he had sent out reached the previously unknown coast. Raleigh's two captains had claimed possession of this "remote barbarous and heathen land not possessed by any Christian prince or people" under a patent issued to Raleigh by the queen. In return, she expected to receive a fifth of whatever precious metals were mined in Virginia.

The colonists left England on April 9, 1585, in five ships commanded by Sir Richard Grenville, an outstanding British admiral who was a cousin of Sir Walter. Following the same route the two exploring ships had taken the year before, the colonists reached their destination on August 17. With great excitement on board, the five ships anchored a safe distance from the strange shore. A few men rowed to the sandy beach, wondering whether the Indians standing there would be friendly or attack them. Through sign language and gifts, it was hoped it might be possible to keep peace.

Among the first to go ashore was Ralph Lane, who was to be governor of the little colony as soon as the governor-general, Sir Richard Grenville, left for England with the fleet. Another was John White, a watercolor artist who later became the grandfather of Virginia Dare—the first English child born in America. Still another was Thomas Hariot, twenty-five years old, who came as surveyor and historian for Virginia. Both White and Hariot were well versed in natural history. Their job would be to help the other colonists choose between the useful and the harmful plants and animals in America.

It is easy to imagine how eagerly Sir Richard Grenville questioned these men each time they returned to his flagship, and how all the other colonists aboard strained their ears to hear the answers.

"How now, gentlemen," Sir Richard may have greeted them. "What is it that ye have learned today from all your bartering and conversing with the savages? Ralph Lane, there, did ye discover how they catch fine fishes to eat where none bite on the baited hooks we lower over the side of the ships?"

"We saw fishes of many kinds, Sir Richard," replied Lane. "The savages take some by hand. Some they trap. Others they spear. In all manners of catching fishes the men are very cunning."

"Their spears are very different from ours," said John White. "Since they have neither iron nor steel nor the knowledge of how to make them, they point their spears with the tail of a fish."

"Gentlemen, gentlemen!" Sir Richard Grenville protested. "Do not jest with me! How could a fish's tail be used to point a spear? Come, now. Let us have facts, not fiction!"

"What John White tells is true enough, Sir Richard," said Thomas Hariot. "The tail they use is that of a very curious kind of fish they call the Se-ekanauk. It is not forked, but a long stiff spine, hollow and strong." He held his hands about nine inches apart to indicate how long the spine was.

"The savages fasten the fish's tail to stiff reeds or to the end of a long rod," Ralph Lane added. "With this point they spear softer fish, both by day and by night."

Sir Richard at first made it clear that he couldn't believe such a story, but all three men seemed to agree on it. "What kind of fish can this be, then?" he demanded.

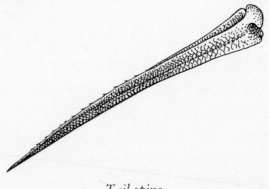

Tail spine

"Show Sir Richard your sketch, John," Thomas Hariot urged.

John White, the artist, opened his sketchbook and held it out. "See how the body is in two parts, with the spiny tail attached on behind. The fish is about a foot wide, has many legs below, and its eyes are set in its back. The savages take them by hand in salt-water shallows or on the shore."

"Gentlemen, gentlemen!" Sir Richard objected. "No fish has legs. Do ye mean fins? And no fish that ever I saw had a shape like that. Is it a fish at all?"

John White answered, "No fish like this comes to the shores of England, Sir Richard. Nor to the Continent either. It is a crusty shellfish, more like a crab than a fish. But it is not a crab either. Its shell has the shape of a horse's hoof, and is almost as hard. If I were to name it, I would call it the Horsefoot Crab."

Thomas Hariot interrupted. "But it is not a crab, John. Crabs have eyes on movable stalks. The Seekanauk has two low bulging eyes embedded in its hard head. And there is another tiny pair in the middle of its forehead. Only the giant Polyphemus in Greek myths had an eye in the middle of his forehead."

Sir Richard Grenville wasn't interested in this argument. Whether the Se-ekanauk was a fish or a crab or something else didn't matter. He changed the subject. "Did ye say that the savages eat these beasts as well as employ their tails for spear points?"

Ralph Lane nodded. "Eat of them they do, Sir Richard. They gave us some, and 'twas tasty food—like a fish stew."

Sir Richard Grenville puckered up his lips. "I doubt me that any proper Englishman would buy one for dinner, since the fish is in such a strange shell. Did ye say that the savages trap the Se-ekanauk or take it only by hand?"

John White opened his notebook, found another sketch and held it for the admiral to see. "They trap the fish, too. Along the shore at intervals they build fences made of poles, driven into the bottom. In the

fences, which extend out from shore, are little rooms entered by a narrow door. The savages are very clever. They build these rooms where a pool of water stays when the tide is out. Then the fishes that are caught in the rooms will live until they can be taken."

When all the colonists had settled ashore, Sir Richard Grenville sailed back to England. He promised to return the following spring with another shipload of supplies. But the colonists had a hard winter. The Indians were treacherous, always ready to attack. The crops grew poorly. June came, and still Sir Richard did not return.

Instead, Sir Francis Drake arrived with twenty-three ships. He had just defeated the Spanish and plundered the forts at Cartagena (Colombia), Santo Domingo (West Indies), and St. Augustine (Florida). He was anxious to help and said he could provide for most of the needs of the colonists. Or, if they preferred, he could take everyone and their possessions to England. Governor Lane and the colonists decided to abandon Virginia and go with Sir Francis. They sailed on June 18, two weeks before Sir Richard Grenville's ships arrived.

To Sir Walter Raleigh in England, Governor Lane took an Indian tobacco pipe and taught him to smoke it. Historian Thomas Hariot carried along his thick notebooks and two of the strangest plants he had encountered in the New World: tobacco and potato. Artist John White went with just his colored sketches—the first ever made to show the people and creatures of America.

Seventy-five of White's original drawings are now in the British Museum, bound together as "The Pictures of Sundry Things Collected and Counterfeited According to the Truth, in the Voyage Made by Sir W. Raleigh, Knight, for the Discovery of La Virginea, in the 27th Year of the Most Happie Reigne of Our Soveraigne Lady Queene Elizabeth." Hariot's decriptions of the Se-ekanauk and the fishing methods of the Indians were published in London during 1588 in his book *A Briefe and True Report of the New Found Land of Virginia.*

To the shores where the Se-ekanauk lived John White returned in 1587. He came as the new governor of the "country" of Virginia, bringing with him 150 colonists. They included his daughter Elinor and his son-in-law Ananias Dare. At the place now known as Roanoke Island, North Carolina, they re-established the British settlement. There his grandchild, Virginia Dare, was born on August 18, just twenty-seven days after the colonists arrived. Fort Raleigh, a national historical site, marks the place today. It is a wild bit of coast, littered with the cast-off shells of horseshoe crabs. They are thrown ashore by the violent storms that have made Cape Hatteras, close by, famous as "the graveyard of ships."

The little colony on Roanoke Island disappeared. So have the Indians who contested the right of Europeans to settle there. But the Se-ekanauks continue to swim in the shallow water, and to clamber out on the edge of the beach when it is the proper season for laying their eggs.

Later settlers found the horseshoe crabs along the whole Atlantic coast, as far north as the Bay of Fundy and Nova Scotia, as far south as the tip of Florida, and around the shores of the Gulf of Mexico to Yucatán. Old books showing the animals of the West Indies portray these same creatures on the coast of Jamaica.

People invented their own names for the Se-ekanauk: swordtail crab, saucepan crab, king crab, piggy-back crab, and horsefoot crab. But somehow, horsefoot became horseshoe crab—the commonest common name wherever these strange creatures are found. Since 1758, the scientists of the world have known the horseshoe crab of America's Atlantic Coast as *Limulus polyphemus*, a name that refers both to the large oval eyes that bulge slightly from the sides of the rounded front part of the body, and also to the tiny eyes in the middle of the forehead. The Latin word *limus* means a sidewise glance.

The west coast of America has no horseshoe crabs. Nor have any shores of South America, Africa, Europe, or Australia. Similar kinds of life exist only far away in the East Indies. As long ago as 1558 a drawing of one of them was published in the book *Historia Animalium* by Joannes Jonstonius. Probably a sea captain brought a dried specimen to Europe from one of the romantic spice islands, the Moluccas. Johnstonius named the drawing *Cancer mollucensis* ("crab of the Moluccas"). He drew the picture without telling anything about the animal. Today there is no way to learn which one of the kinds that live there he actually drew.

Three kinds of horseshoe crab are now found along the shores of the East Indies and Southeast Asia: one (*Tachypleus gigas*) from Singapore to the Torres Straits between New Guinea and Australia; another (*Tachypleus tridentatus*) from around the Sea of Japan and the South China Sea; and the third (*Carcinoscorpius rotundicauda*) from the coasts of Burma, past Singapore and the Philippine Islands to Japan and the adjacent shores of China. All three are slightly smaller than the Se-ekanauks of America. But all have a similar shape and habits. All possess some amazing secret for survival.

Perhaps the horseshoe crab's secret is in moderation and modest versatility. It never goes far into the fresh water of the rivers, or far down into the salty ocean. Close to the coast and protected by an armored shell, it meets few creatures that can do it harm. For food it can use almost any small animal living in the top inch or two of the mud and sand that accumulate on the sea bottom. It makes no difference that the first kinds of creatures on which the crabs fed became extinct. There have always been

substitutes of some kind for horseshoe crabs to eat. With such simple needs, these amazing animals have been able to crawl at a leisurely pace out of the distant past into modern times.

Looking Into the Future

By CRAWLING OUT of the past into the present, horseshoe crabs have given themselves a future. But for any animal, the future is always full of danger. The crabs that lived on while the dinosaurs became extinct have met a new and more influential neighbor: mankind. In recent years man has become far more dangerous than the dinosaurs ever were. Man is changing the world of the horseshoe crabs so fast that their future may be far shorter than their past. Their leisurely ways may not let them keep up with the rapid changes.

In the Far East, these "living fossils" are in much less danger than in North America. Along the coasts of Asia and the East Indies, the people still catch horseshoe crabs to eat. But their fishing methods are inefficient and the number of crabs that get caught is fairly small.

The crabs in the Far East are endangered by man today only to about the same extent that they were in America before colonists arrived from Europe. Along the Atlantic Coast, the Indians did little to reduce the total number of crabs. There simply weren't enough Indians to matter. The crabs reproduced far faster than the Indians caught them to eat their eggs and meat, or to get their tails for hard points to attach to spears and arrows. Among the weapons that have been dug from Indian mounds and burial sites, only a few are tipped with the tails of horseshoe crabs. The others bear tips of flint or bone or eagle claws or pieces of antler from deer. Farther from the coast, the Indians had no tails of horseshoe crabs at all.

After 1600, the colonists from Europe swiftly replaced the Indians along shores to which the crabs came at mating season. But the new Americans acted as though they agreed completely with Sir Richard Grenville's view: "I doubt me that any proper

Englishman would buy one for dinner, since the fish is in such a strange shell!" Although better spears and better nets for catching fish were available, the use of horseshoe crabs for human food ceased for lack of interest.

The fishermen of European descent were eager to catch the cod, the shad, the ocean perch, and the croaker. But when they hauled their nets along the bottom to get these fishes, they caught many a horseshoe crab as well. The crabs made the net heavy, straining it and also crushing the valuable fishes. The tails and projecting corners of the shells caught on the nets and tore them. Or the crabs got so entangled in the meshes that the fishermen had to spend hours in removing the animals by hand. None of this added to the popularity of horseshoe crabs.

First the coastal settlers discovered that both their domesticated pigs and chickens would clean the meat from a horseshoe crab if its armored shell was cut open. For pigs, each live crab was simply chopped into quarters. For chickens, a man with a knife separated the legs and under armor from the whole upper part of the crab. It then became worthwhile to go after horseshoe crabs, to make pigs and chickens grow faster, producing meat for man. Thousands of crabs were soon used in this way.

Next, people along the coast learned that dried crabs could be made into fertilizer that would make plants grow faster. To capture crabs by the million, fishermen began building fences of poles and chicken-wire netting. The fences, called "hedges," stretched straight out from shore into fairly deep water. Gradually the design of these traps improved until they were almost the same as the ones John White sketched in 1586. The Indians had built as good traps for horseshoe crabs as anybody could!

Each time the tide went out, the fishermen visited their traps and removed the crabs. If any useful fish happened to get caught, too, the gain was that much greater. The men put the crabs in pens made of chicken wire high on the shore and left them to die of thirst in the hot sun. The dead crabs were stacked to shed the rain until they dried completely. Dried crabs were ground up to make the fertilizer. But much of the good in them was lost because flies laid eggs on the dead crabs and the worms that hatched ate out the meat inside them. A dry crab might be only a shell, with little real value as fertilizer.

In the middle of the nineteenth century, the harvesting of horseshoe crabs reached its peak. Along the Cape May shore of Delaware Bay, as many as 1,200,000 of them were collected in 1856 from a single mile of coast. Only a few people protested so shameful an end for so strange an animal. The population of horseshoe crabs grew less and less.

In the late 1920's, the total number of horseshoe crabs caught along the whole Atlantic Coast of America fell to about 5 million a year. In the 1930's it was 4 million; in the 1940's 3 million, then 2, and only 1; in the 1950's the fishery fell to a quarter of a million crabs; in the 1960's it came to an end. Statistics on it are no longer kept.

Horseshoe crabs grow at too leisurely a pace to be harvested heavily. The fishermen ruined their own fishing by being greedy. Yet the end might not have come so quickly if other people had not helped change the world for horseshoe crabs. These people, in coastal cities, built boat docks and sea walls along the shores to which the animals once came to mate and lay eggs. People gave no thought to crabs when they built garbage dumps on land that had no other human use. But their garbage supported a far larger number of sea gulls than lived along the coast before 1920. Between meals on garbage, the gulls ate young horseshoe crabs on the mud flats and sand bars. Fewer crabs survived to search along the shore for an unspoiled place to mate and dig a nest.

American horseshoe crabs are not extinct—not

yet. In some places, the sports fishermen along the shore wish they were. The men regard the crabs as bad for their sport. Because the crabs eat sea worms close to shore, the fishes have less to eat there. The fishes stay in deeper water where the fishermen cannot catch them so easily.

Shell fishermen, too, complain that the crabs eat young clams and oysters, reducing the number that are available to man. But the damage is so slight and the coastal shellfish beds often so poor that no one gives serious thought to ridding the coast of crabs altogether.

Only a small number of people have looked for other good in horseshoe crabs. Perhaps the first to do so were the Indians on Martha's Vineyard, an island close to the shore of Cape Cod. These Indians strung on their necklaces the special fist-and-claw pincers of male horseshoe crabs. They may have been good-luck charms.

Today scientists are discovering about life by studying horseshoe crabs. These animals are the blue bloods of the Animal Kingdom. Not only is their ancestry well known for many years and generations, but their blood is actually blue. The color comes from a substance called *hemocyanin*, which has copper in it. It helps carry oxygen in the blood, much as does hemoglobin, which is the red coloring material in human blood.

In its blue blood, the crab may have hidden one of the secrets of its survival through so many millions of years. Almost no bacteria will grow in the blood of a horseshoe crab. It seems to contain its own kind of antibiotic medicine. No one knows yet whether this substance can be used to help treat sicknesses in people. It would be a great loss to have horseshoe crabs become extinct before scientists discover how they are protected from disease bacteria.

Human lives have already been saved because of information learned from horseshoe crabs. The nervous connections in the heart and in the compound eyes of the crab are far simpler than those in a human being's heart and eyes. Yet the way the nerves control the heartbeat of the crab and the way the nerves carry messages from its eyes to its brain are remarkably similar to the same processes in man. By studying how the simpler system operates in a crab, scientists can devise ways to help people.

Somewhere in the nervous connections to its compound eyes and brain, the crab has a different secret to which man would like the answer. The crab can tell the time of day, even if it is kept in a dark room. Using its mysterious inner "clock," it can steer a course in the sea or on land according to the changing pattern of light from the sky. No one knows where the "clock" lies inside the animal, or even just what to look for. Yet some soft tissue close to the brain must have this strange role. By learning how it operates, scientists might be able to apply the principle to human needs.

Today the harvest of information and ideas from the study of horseshoe crabs is far more important than the use of their armored bodies for food or fertilizer. These animals are living museums, full of the secrets of survival. Few of man's animal neighbors can compare with these crabs that crawled out of the past in offering a wealth of experience from which mankind can benefit.

Index

Lorus J. Milne and Margery Milne, professors and exploring scientists, have worked together since their college days. They have lectured at a number of universities together, and their travels have taken them over 300,000 miles through four continents.

Lorus J. Milne was born in Toronto, Canada, and is now a citizen of the United States. He attended the University of Toronto, where he was named a Gold Medalist for his work in biology. He received his Ph.D. from Harvard University.

Margery Milne, a native of New York City, attended Columbia University and received her M.A. and Ph.D. from Radcliffe College.

The Milnes are the authors of many books, among them one other book for children, *Because of a Tree*. Of it *The American Biology Teacher* said, "The Milnes have done a masterful job of developing for youngsters the ecologists's theme of a 'balanced community'." Among the many adult books the Milnes have written are: *Paths Across the Earth, Animal Life, Plant Life, The Balance of Nature, The Senses of Animals and Men,* and *Water and Life.*